TOOLS FOR TEACHERS

- **ATOS:** 0.7
- **GRL:** A
- **LEXILE:** BR50L

- **CURRICULUM CONNECTIONS:** opposites, sorting, temperature
- **WORD COUNT:** 56

Skills to Teach

- **HIGH-FREQUENCY WORDS:** cold, hot, is, this, what
- **CONTENT WORDS:** child, drink, forest, sandwich, treat, water
- **PUNCTUATION:** periods, question marks
- **WORD STUDY:** /ng/, spelled n (*drink*); r-controlled vowels (*forest, water*); long /e/, spelled ea (*treat*); multisyllable words (*forest, sandwich, water*)
- **TEXT TYPE:** compare/contrast

Before Reading Activities

- Read the title and give a simple statement of the main idea.
- Have students "walk" though the book and talk about what they see in the pictures.
- Introduce new vocabulary by having students predict the first letter and locate the word in the text.
- Discuss any unfamiliar concepts that are in the text.

After Reading Activities

Write the book's language pattern on the board: "This_____ is hot." in one column, and "This_____is cold." in another. Encourage children to think about things that are hot and things that are cold, as well as things that can be either hot or cold depending on the conditions. Write their answers under the appropriate column.

Tadpole Books are published by Jump!, 5357 Penn Avenue South, Minneapolis, MN 55419, www.jumplibrary.com

Copyright ©2018 Jump. International copyright reserved in all countries. No part of this book may be reproduced in any form without written permission from the publisher.

Editor: Jenny Fretland VanVoorst **Designer:** Anna Peterson

Photo Credits: Alamy: Doug Schneider, 4. Shutterstock: MaraZe, cover; Ninell, cover; Vadim.Petrov, cover; Littlekidmoment, 1; macro-vectors, 2; nalinratphi, 2; phokin, 2–3; Africa Studio, 3; Olga Miltsova, 6; espies, 6–7; Denis Tabler, 7; Jaye Thompson, 8; tarapong srichaiyos, 8; tanatat, 9; Vibrant Image Studio, 10; Vitalii_Mamchuk, 11; agusyonok, 12; JeniFoto, 13; Arina P Habich, 14, 15. SuperStock: Tetra Images, 5.

Library of Congress Cataloging-in-Publication Data
Names: Donner, Erica, author.
Title: Hot and cold / by Erica Donner.
Description: Minneapolis, MN: Jump!, Inc., (2017) | Series: Opposites | Audience: Ages 3–6. | Includes index.
Identifiers: LCCN 2016057772 (print) | LCCN 2017005775 (ebook) | ISBN 9781620317525 (hardcover: alk. paper) | ISBN 9781620317723 (pbk.) | ISBN 9781624965999 (ebook)
Subjects: LCSH: Heat—Juvenile literature. | Polarity—Juvenile literature.
Classification: LCC QC256 .D66 2017 (print) | LCC QC256 (ebook) | DDC 536—dc23
LC record available at https://lccn.loc.gov/2016057772

OPPOSITES

HOT AND COLD

by Erica Donner

TABLE OF CONTENTS

tadpole
books

HOT AND COLD

This water is hot.

water

This water is cold.

This child is hot.

This child is cold.

This sandwich is hot.

sandwich

This sandwich is cold.

This treat is hot.

This treat is cold.

This forest is hot.

This forest is cold.

This drink is hot.

This drink is cold.

What else is hot?

What else is cold?

WORDS TO KNOW

child

drink

forest

sandwich

treat

water

INDEX